HEARTBEATS
IN STONES

HEARTBEATS
IN STONES

POEMS I PAM USCHUK

NEW PALTZ · NEW YORK

ACKNOWLEDGEMENTS

JOURNALS

Another Chicago Magazine: The Horseman of the Crass and Vulnerable Word
Asheville Poetry Review: We Thought No One Could See Us
Nimrod: A Dream, My Child
Pequod: With Its Toll of Char
Peregrine: In the Egyptian Rooms
Poetry: Meditations Beside Kootenai Creek
Rattapallax: Fighting the Cold
Tendril: Through the Dark, A Brilliance
Zone: Wildflowers

ANTHOLOGIES

Bridges: Poets of the Hudson Valley: With Its Toll of Char
Only in Her Shoes: Wildflowers

My gratitude goes to my dear friends, Lynn Watt who illustrated the cover, Donley Watt who suggested the title for the book, and Mary Ann Campau and Emilie George for their faith in me and their invaluable help in proofing the text. Thanks also to Bryce Milligan publisher of Wings Press who generously allowed the reprinting of "Through the Dark, A Brilliance" and "Smooth Razor" from the collection, *Finding Peaches in the Desert*. I am grateful to Felicia Rice and Moving Parts Press for their special edition broadside of "A Dream, My Child," accompanied by the original woodcut, "Whose Dream?" by Miriam Rice. Finally, but never lastly, I am deeply grateful for the presence of Bill Root in my life and for making many of these poems possible.

THIS IS A CHAPBOOK
PUBLISHED BY CODHILL PRESS

ISBN 1-930337-17-5

Book design by Carla Rozman
Cover design by Lynn Watt

Manufactured in the United States of America.
First Edition.

DEDICATION

This collection is dedicated with love and ravens and whitewater
laughter to my favorite poet, friend and love, Bill Root,
and to Val and Max to keep their heartbeats strong.

CONTENTS

THROUGH THE DARK, A BRILLIANCE
for Judi and Val

You always think the untended will fail
                like the amaryllis
left for months in a dark bedroom.
And it is deserved
if its leaves turn brown and it slumps
around its pot, not like the rose
you dutifully prune,
pinching off dead blossoms
to make way for the new.
The rose you believe is immortal,
a Lazarus you guard so close
the petals blind you to the roots, the way
they rot in floods underground.
When it finally dies, despite
fertilizers, the patient attention
to blooms, you wonder
why it reminds you of love
whose showiness promises
the illusion you sustain,
not wanting to know what navigates there
like blind fish in subterranean streams.

Then, you remember the amaryllis,
                its own shepherdess,
who even now sprouts the stalk
whose bud will become
the trumpeting blossom, a brilliance
that is a surprise sustaining itself
through months of dark and mysterious longings
your careful hands would learn.

THE HORSEMAN OF THE CRASS
AND VULNERABLE WORD
For J.H.

The hemlock loses the tanager,
a bright blood streak
in a whirling gauze of snow.
Where do we go?
You told me the eye was lost,
old lens in a dish of milk
going to blue-veined cheese,
a lens that sneezed
when you laughed the mockingbird's laugh,
the horse's white laugh,
saying your brother accidentally
shot it out as you crawled
under barb wire, hunting.

I was young and fell in love
with your wounds, your tongue,
half-song, half-glands,
strong as the Calvinist hands
that whacked and fed your swampy youth.
I was young and drank vermouth
while you fell to your knees
in the Ford's back seat where you teased
until I laughed too much
when you begged please,
and your one-eyed touch
stared up at the night jar sky,
blinked at Orion, your
archer, saying good-bye.
I laughed but I feared your tongue,
your thighs. I was young.
I had heard.
Never love a poet at his word.
You were the man who could maim me
in those days when whiskey

clarified any dark thing.
Like Bobby and Annette we'd sing,
Baby, you're my beach blanket;
I'm your Mickey Mouse coquette.

You knew my crippled heart, my blind side
but I'd ride ride
on that edge where the heart's not given,
can't be taken
or lost to an archer or poet with one eye.
Oh, the heart has a spongy hide
believing in love's bromide.
Mine found its bed unmade, undone
when you left with your joking tongue.

But I tell you this now,
horseman of the crass and vulnerable word,
love is damp as a cloud-blown beach
and crawls in your bones
that never lose their ache.
When I dreamed your face—
so blindly polite, just the glimpse
of a lens of a face, just before
the horse, the dark and slippery horse I rode
so far out to sea
that the shore was a crumb the gulls couldn't eat—
I went numb in my sleep.
Even numbness passes.
I am half-blind in this half-blind night
but I've learned to ferment
wine from ash.
And you, it's always late—
you've broken your horse,
now lie under it.

WITH ITS TOLL OF CHAR
after hearing Ted Hughes read

All sounds bassoon in haze.
Trees stretch shoulder deep
in fog breathing up from the slow river,
where the courting of frogs booms
under the moon's waning halo.
To vague stars turning over sky, black limbs
hold up their devotion of autumn leaves.
Inside midnight's sleeve
the architecture of imagination slips
from its routine mooring
in an earthquake of dreams, and the car
jars you awake
as I skid to miss the fox
sniffing its mate dead on the freeway.

What shapes irony? Coming home
late from the City after the Laureate's story
of the fox-faced man who peeked at him from the kitchen door,
then placed his charred hands over his poems,
I start at the overwhelming red tail
as it brushes the rushing bumper.

This fox is real.
It's dangerous, you say, *to swerve
for animals caught on the ice.*

Event becomes myth. How
often we drift, safe in our faith
something will get us home alive,
though we risk everything.
        Night gathers details we forget.
What it says comes true.
In fog, frogs never give up their insistent courting,
and stars chart careful courses to dawn.

In the unkempt church of desire,
sometimes we pray for flame
that becomes its own fuel
charging the heart with its toll of char.

That fox must have watched his mate cross the pavement
like a stream parting their known woods
in the nightly routine of their hunt.
What he couldn't name split her side, flipping her once
as he snapped at the monstrous shape
even as it was swallowed wholly by dark.

The fox might have started sooner
from my oncoming car, but he stood
taking in her scent a last time
that commonplace night
none of us could any longer take for granted
as his red fur ignited, guard hairs
flaming spikes

MEDITATIONS BESIDE KOOTENAI CREEK
For Bill

I

Sometimes I become what I least desire,
old as bone, uncomprehending
as the memory of pain.
Perhaps dusk comes into a room
and a woman rattles up
out of my throat, her eyes
empty as candles set aside for the dead
who no longer care for such light,
her flesh gone to the birds.
It is then
in gray light, she tells me
my skin sags, my heart is incomplete in its beatings.
I haven't learned to love
as much as the stars
who are at least not cruel.
Then, as if in a dream of fire along a foggy ridge,
I walk out,
hands sprouting green flames,
eyes not blind enough from blue smoke,
and I hear
from its sad shadow in wet grass
the sudden up-cry of a meadowlark
and I believe I will never be alone again.

II

Listening to the wild applause of water
as it clarifies rocks we step across,
we hear what we'd name,
Western Tanager,
Song Sparrow,

Lazuli Bunting,
and over a silver patch of river, dim
in cedar shadows, the thick bilious
laughter of ravens.

You say,
Walk in cold water.
Let it burn your feet.

When you dive into the stream
you float for a while, then try to
hold the current in your pale hands,
and I remember your fingers
like coals stoking my breasts.

Your black hair waves like tentacles
or a negative halo radiant in its aquamarine pool.
Like blind minnows, your fingertips
bump the smooth skulls of stones underwater,
and, for a moment, I worry you'll drown.
But you rise, streaming
a chandelier of watery light
even our dark sides love.

Last night I dreamed of blood and beatings,
of giving away a bright red slip.
I tied my mother to a gypsy wagon and drove it West,
while her arms like kites
waved at passing weeds she blessed. Over
and over she asked,
> *If the eye is blue as beach glass,*
> *will it see itself*
> *leap to the bottom of the stream?*

I watch a water ouzel now
whose name you won't believe.
It dips in and out of sizzling foam,
its thin yellow legs canny
on moss-covered stones I'd slip on.
I watch it disappear beneath white water
consuming itself above the bird
who emerges sky-gray, triumphant on the opposite shore.

III

Ordeal by ice—
    twice, twice
    I'd change my heart to ice,
    suspend it twice in air
    to sprout wings for the wind's care,
    then cage it in the bones of flame
    to unlock the twins from separate names.

Even as a young girl, I'd sit
beside a dry creek I'd wish was full
and sketch the tanager, shading
black wings on its heart-red sides.

Sitting alone under the vast
loneliness of trees in that small woods,
I heard voices huge with wind
and the coming dusk that wouldn't let me go.

Who could I tell but the dead?
What name could I give passion?
I watched the way animals surprised the grass
then I pretended I was a lion
no one could kill.

Summer's demise—
>   *Gemini rises just before*
>   *midnight in the southern sky.*
>   *Castor and Pollux,*
>   *from icy toe to icy toe,*
>   *I'd trace with a twin's eye for balance.*
>   *Even the dead must have this simple joy.*

IV

After all these years, what we come to,
wet branches beating our chests as we wade
to the other side of the creek.
Reaching for the slippery knuckles of roots
clinging to clay banks, we fall
into water we can see through.
Cedar perfumes our numb fingers
that finally hold musky bark.
How deliciously we shiver.

This is the journey the heart makes,
back through water, under stars
filled with the certainty of submarine light.
We count the times we've drowned to live.

When I climb ashore, you splash
water straight into the air at my feet.
This time I can love and shove away the dead.
You splash again.
It is that simple. I wait
for the ouzel to come back downstream,
wait for its small piping,
your splashing already deep inside me.

PLANTING TIGRITAS AFTER SNOW IN APRIL

Like a Lear jet out of control, wind shears,
slicing from Silverton ice fields, rattles
even indignant ravens from
the frigid chandelier of the blue spruce.
Down the block a goshawk blows like a kite
almost inside out in a gust
that thrusts its cold fists down my sore throat.

But I am an optimist, plant twenty-five
Tigrita bulbs, those open-mouthed spotted lilies
I hope will roar near stunted tulips
and those daffodils nursing bad self-concepts
that refuse to bud. Mid-April
and still we shiver like slim copper rose twigs
banging the bedroom window.

Hard gardening here in the Rockies
reminds me of tending the irregular seasons
of a long marriage, replacing rotted bulbs, adding
fertilizer to depleted earth, watering
frail stems and pruning back resentment
that blights healthy green stems.

Take off your gloves. Kneel
and dig into stony ground, loosen
dirt compacted by months of incessant snow,
each fingernail gleaming like a saucy black moon.
Feel the shape of each root, the way it sucks
nutrients from mulch you pat around each tender shoot
to protect it against wind, hail, late killer frost.

By July your yard will be nothing
but a jungle of color so entranced, lightning
and thunder will only intensify
the muscular paws of these rearing tigers
you've coaxed from the cold shoulder of the world.

A DREAM, MY CHILD

When in the thrift store
I found that child's satin dress,
its miniature sleeves opening
the air like lilac scent, I thought
of you who so often in dreams
swim in a quick release
of dark water from my inner thighs.
There is no pain, only a rush
rocking like a tide reversing.
Your head is slick with black hair
and you do not scream at displacement
but lie with glowing eyes.

You have remained a dream, my child,
and as often as I have held you
nursing above the tightness
in my womb, I have awakened startled but warm.
If there is anything
I can tell you now, it is that
I bought that dress, knowing
its folded wings may never open.
It lies with eyes shut
in violet light among my clothes.

My child, you have become
the words that discover breath across
the empty pages, an imperfection of longing
whose arrival is incredible.

PEELING THE KITCHEN

Talk about exfoliation. This archaeology will
take me weeks. First comes the ripping, then
total destruction.
                    Wrenching out
screeching nails with crow bars,
we pry huge sheets of cheap paneling
from the old walls to reveal
the smoky history of paint, and under
        that, a century of wall papers shed
like snake skins embossed on rough sandstone.

Who chose the bottom pattern tattooed
with blue and red flowers or the pink sky
speckled with gold stars, tiny and multitudinous as fleas?
Beneath everything, the harsh ash-smeared
plaster is the logic that holds.

Like an argument that spirals out of control,
my husband and I cannot stop tearing.
The white insulating ceiling
that we've despised for years must go, so
with our bare fingers, we pull it
crashing with its load of coal soot onto our heads.

When the ceiling lies at our feet, what is there
but more dingy ochre paint over paper, stars
blurred dusty as the distant Pleiades, a silver filigree
some wife may have chosen to mimic moonlight
bathing her spinning head while she sweated
over meals and dishes, waddled with her pregnant belly
back and forth between woodstove and table, where
her silver miner sat to slurp her rich soup.

Day after day, I mount the rickety ladder
to avoid my computer, where I should compose
poems that shake their fists at stars or hold
the fevered heads of children in distant warring lands.

It is comforting this peeling back,
the scraper prying up paint chips
the size of communion wafers
while I balance on precarious steps scraping,
the motion repetitive as prayer.

Where all the sweet conformity of yellow
        pastel as chilled butter
once soothed our kitchen, strange maps
of foreign planets bloom, a diasphora of galaxies
blasted into this burnished and variegated watershed.

Perhaps, then this simple work is poetry, to scrape
back chaotic layers of buried patterns
with their stories, charting
the way love, betrayal
and faith create history's light and awful web.

CAREER MOVE

Dulled by office duties, the deadpan clutter
of my desk, committee e-mails with
no feet for rhythm, I doze like the weed-caked croc
offshore, watching for any slight stir
a furred foot dipped in shallows
might create. In dreams I lick
the golden stomach of the girl I was
and the thigh of the woman I want
to be, stretched like sand dunes
heaped by wind's sunburned hands.
I leak from each bureaucratic arrow shot
into hide that thickens over my heart until
no one hears the ruined thud inside
my chest, the need raw as ore
beneath earth's firm crust.
Whoever glimpses me in this buzzing swamp
might fear these yellow eyes
the electric tint of lemon sweat. Look
closer and note how I take
lessons from a showy great egret, whose wings
benevolent as the courtesan's unfolding robes
reach up, then lift from
their reflection warped by stagnant water.

GEOMETRY LESSON

Just as the universe shifts to sketch
a new map of stars from the heart
of gases bent around particles zapped
from black holes that would destroy them
so, falling in love, we invent lips
on the exact curve of the neck
most vulnerable to an axe handle blow,
lips we hope won't construct a triangle of lies.

We outline the angles of hands
the way we'd sculpt
our favorite dough--firm, hot and slow.
Love we revise from
the heart's disasters, fists
pounding the midnight door of fear,
the crazy laughter of flies that
      ferry betrayal on their jeweled wings,
even the ashes of our belief in our failure
to survive. Love divides
or multiplies wet postulates of desire.

Foolishness and trust nuzzle
passion's womb. Balance is axiomatic.
                Twenty years of falling in love
solves twenty years of hanging over the edge.
Twenty years of fire demand
twenty years of water to swelter the flames.
What is the tender palm without the tough skeleton
forming the back of the hand
that can withstand ice
or unrelenting heat
as it calculates the fault lines of the heart?

SMOOTH RAZOR

Wasn't I once the party darling, lion-
haired blonde that flung gold arms
and thighs wild dancing,
yet so shy sometimes and scared
I couldn't tell the truth to anyone
but thickets of wild wrens and trilliums.
When the music stopped, wasn't I the big-eyed doe
who ran from men and boys,
        their terrible baby-laced sex
or the vamp who fell into some stoned bed, moaning
to the pounding surf in my temples,
riding deeper and deeper into suicidal light
the wet horse of need?

Now orange blossoms blow sweet nothings
across the lawn. All the fawn-dappled clouds
paw desert mountains surrounding us,
and I recall how once I snorted into the shock of wind
rimming Grand Traverse Bay at forty below
while the thousand shattering panes of blue ice
piled skyscraper high against the shore,
and I prayed for love, *cherish is the word*
impossible love to save me, for love's
chrome semi grill to crash into me,
a pure ratchet of light
cracking my young marriage-sledged brain, love
sharp and clean as gin,
an obsidian scalpel of love,
love's electrocuted smile,
any love from any lips anywhere.

        But nothing
showed up besides hangovers
and my husband's frigid hands,
his whiskeyed Irish breathing,

his catjumps away from embrace. His constant casting
into cold runs for lunker trout to show the boys
he, too, was one of them, could
joke about tits, wine, his waders
pulled down to dry by his wife. His doomsday drum
snare-rattled the too late world, all hope
shot full of holes as any Belfast street.

Is it any wonder I leapt
        far into the charred arms of distances? Into
the buffalo dreams
of travel, crossing and
recrossing the continent
in a beatup green Impala, alone
except for my sweet mongrel, Ivan,
rug-sprawled across the back seat and demanding nothing
but the soft stroke and ruffle of love between his ears,
along his golden spine.

        Leapt into the anonymous rumples of lovers
who bolted, stung by the tail of love's long-strung syllable.
        Leapt finally into the black-haired arms
of the man my ex-husband warned was a smooth razor.

A razor was my desire
for this man hunkered like a grizzly,
his dark size topped by a mind precise as any Swiss hand
at work over the guts of a watch, mind
that could vault, soaring
like a Marsh Hawk surveying the tangle of swamp and field
updrafted with celestial light,
mind sweet as dark chocolate smeared
across a Mediterranean cheek, Corsican mind
blown in a sudden gust ridiculous
as a dragon kite turned inside out, spinning.

And didn't we spin? We were
two gale-force winds across the globe
bashing into one another, lifting
one another over oceans
and jungles, deserts
and valleys, onto the backs of sweating horses
and their flat-out heart-burst gallop
through bee-buzzed sage.
Our laughter never aged. In movies
or over the comic page
we laughed against black fangs of doubt,
death's dumb fingers
that tried to strangle our verse.

Nearly two decades, we've leapt
into chocolate-covered orange rinds, raspberry pies
and midnight fights,
love bites and cross-country flights
to the biggest Apple
          and back. You always
come back
          to my lips, my hands, my thighs, tangling
your fingers in my hair.
          To the stink of roses
slicking the bedside lamp.

Now, here I sit, eating a whole bag of potato chips
again, not caring to calculate what weight
they'll add to thigh and waist.
Wondering just how the far-flung future
caught up with us, I lick
from my fingertips, salt, sweet
and lovely grease, then lean to your lips.
Handsome healing blade,
we're in it for the long-term kiss.

BELL NOTE

Like a bassoon dropped to the bottom of Lake Michigan
your voice returns in the rain that reduces the world
to amorphous cold smoke I cannot shape.
Shape was never indistinct in your hands that
sculpted everything from kitchen cabinets to built-in beds
and writing desks; those fleshy lathes as
tough and heated as steel poured into molds
for car frames you lifted at the Olds, where you
put in more years than I have teeth
to bite through the stinging barbwire of loneliness
that binds my heart. I recall Sunday
morning phone calls, our bad singing
and your war stories better than any church-
bound sermons, laughter huge as any savior
that brought me back from tightrope walks
across those myriad ice bridges of self-doubt
swayed by disillusionment's raw wind.

Sometimes, Dad, there is no loneliness
like an ad for the Superbowl,
all those coach's blunders you'd cuss out
or the lies of politicians on TV
smiling as they stagger like possums
on the sides of reason's highway.

Remember driving cross-country year
after year from Michigan to Colorado, the Cutlass
a waxed pendulum ticking to the rhythm of your stories—
the way Johnny Weismuller taught you to swim
in ninth grade or the time you flew the bomber
all the way across the Atlantic from Brazil
to the coast of Africa, spread gold
as a lioness against a gigantic wash of blue—
stories to keep each other awake
as we sucked orange wedges, licked
Snickers bars from our fingertips

numbed on the humming wheel.

What did you say to Mom, who sat
knitting or reading in the back seat, when
she'd startle like a rock dove, head
jerking up and away to fly at us with her shriek,
"We're going the wrong way!
That field's on fire. It's heading
right for us!" Maybe her delusions knew
the fire was always heading for us. Today

is your birthday, Dad, and what heads
for me is memory's long smolder
damp as a campfire
on a star-spidered Michigan beach
where somewhere offshore your voice bells
from its submarine cave,
my forgotten loved daughter's name.

THE EGYPTIAN ROOMS
for Joy Harjo and Audle

Who can separate the paired falcons, memory
from imagination, can split the sky.
Too close to flesh tone, I never liked pink stone,
especially granite with its graphite veins
like the varicose headstone on my grandparents' grave.
This museum altar crowds other
displays to the edges of the room.   Stroking
its sacrificial trough, electric
as forbidden skin, once again I'm hurled back.

Our black eyes were shaded
blue, novices raised in the same temple room.
Gold ringed our necks, ankles,
our bird-boned wrists. We laughed at
our chests unflattening themselves.

One desert noon a falcon screamed
at our window just before the priest
carried in his bitter pack of leaves
to slip between our teeth.
When he lifted his white robe
for the stiff initiation, I found my foot
and refused with a perfect kick.
Anger like white knuckles
tightened his face as he thrust
the knife through my terrified ribs.
I'd tell you it was painless
beyond the blade, but for you
the room ached like a split womb.

How much of memory is will? We are still
the same laughter, bodies
slim as deer, story-telling
fingers ringed by shields—
                    silver, lapis,

turquoise and gold—
with their histories of wounds and needs.

How often have we died young, sacrificed
for love or lust? Sometimes
I dream wide, of a river ripe with crocodiles
or a lion deciphering the dusky musk of reeds.
Who would believe
the strange worlds of desire
that whirl in my sleep?

This morning when you dizzied in the staggering space
between skyscrapers on the way to the Met,
I heard them speak.

Now all of it rockets back—
how my dead flesh married stone
while you laced the jade frog
on the leather thong around my neck.
Tears worried your angel dark face
searching for my voice that thinned
above the altar where I never learned to pray.
Inconsolable days you arranged
orange trumpet flowers in my hair
until your tears were blades
that sliced the priest's drugged throat.

Two thousand years later we enter this passage way
lined with mummies behind glass.
Their anger bites the hemostatic air.
I can almost see them breathe.
Who's to say which catalogue
of sacred wounds is real?
Furious for balance we lean
against one another's temporary form.

You hold your hand over the songbird
of your heart tossing in terrible wind.
Hold onto me when we return
to the traffic-jazzed streets,
the blind blotters of skyscraper windows,
all the rushed faces who won't meet our eyes.

We are dangerous, hot
as smuggled knives. How short
the time. We are smoke
from funeral flames, rising
cold and pure as the language of stars.

LAUNDRY LIST ON THE BACK OF A MAPLE LEAF

After the eclipsed moon's full howl, how
strange the plunge and lift of autumn
temperatures that mimic the knees
of a girl first testing ocean surf
with her perfumed feet before
her headlong dive to end her dreams.
Flame takes the sky
on the last Indian summer wind
reeking of diesel
from construction across the street,
a fire ant wind biting us
to believe we've flipped
the calendar of our hearts back to June bugs
and a chigger-clogged sun, except
we can't miss the branches
as bare as our longing to hold
this last warmth against ice rains
that will maim us, freeze
our joints, shatter
our sex inside
their teary rictus.
           Frost's rigid fingers crack
the lips of fall dawns
just as sun snaps like a black seed on fire
over the horizon and the blue heron unhinges
its death-colored wings.

This could be the last day on earth,
day rung by rusted clappers of goodbye,
the salt of loneliness smeared
down time's crenellated spine,
a dog regarding the Vet's needle
that will put her down, the last cry
of the premature lamb
secured in the coyote's teeth,
crocodile smile of the lover
planting his betrayal in a handful of dirt,
a chipped tooth of grief.
In window urns and gardens
all over town, winter cabbages
replace the last defiant blooms.

ON ANY DESERT SUNDAY MORNING

Before rose-scorch, before butterflies
hide in the clipped leaves
of citrus, before
the sexslam of coffee and the buttery traffic
of croissants, I believe
in the arms of dreamfall and longings
dug from love's sleeping sternum
as I watch your buffalo shoulders
turn under the swirling fan,
before waking, the ache of morning
sweet as dove croon and finch,
as dew not yet bruised by the same blast of light
that defines the cool shadows of our lives.

SAVING THE CORMORANT CAUGHT IN A GILL NET ON ALBEMARLE SOUND

Like a photographic image licked to life
in a chemical bath, chill light
defines the dawning world with shadows
that bruise the silver cheek of the sound
as we pack the canoe for a trek
into the Great Dismal Swamp.

Paddling past the ghosts of drowned cypress
I focus on a pair of cormorants a hundred feet offshore.
One startles skyward eaten by fog while
the other slingshots up then slams
back into rising chop. What monster
would stake out a bird in rising tide?
To set it loose we paddle hard, not
considering the problems wind
and our two wolf-dogs pose, noses
testing sea scents from mid-canoe.

Fog silent we glide near enough to see
the net hung with irresistible underwater jewelry—
fat sea bass flapping against polystyrene
strung mean as a political lie
halfway across the bay's wide grin.
Diving through tea-colored currents, even
the cormorant's keen night sight
couldn't detect plastic's fatal invisibility.

When you lean to free the snarled bird
as big as a black swan, the screeching orange beak
and terrible machine gun slaps
of its one free wing whack your hand,
shoulder and unprotected head.
Both dogs leap and we rock wild,
nearly pitching into frigid surf.
Over the heaving fists of my heartbeats

I can no longer hear our screams
for the dogs to lie still.

Each time you reach over the bobbing gunnel
to slice a tough link with a small fillet knife,
its hooked beak strikes, tattoos
bruises through your thin leather glove
until you grasp the muscular neck.

We are as precarious as we've ever been
and know that if we swamp we'll freeze
before we can make it to shore, but neither of us
was ever meant to quit.   Those set-jawed wills
that hopelessly mire us in arguments, now
bite through fear knotting our chests.

While you struggle not to hurt the frantic bird
I inch the canoe bow to the only
stable point I see, then grab
the punky trunk that threatens to disintegrate,
hugging this illusion for all of us that toss
on a trampoline of rising surf.

Holding the netted aloft, you hack
one strand at a time, but with each slash
the cormorant thrashes, tangling deeper
in the Chinese puzzle of gill nets
until we lose faith. Whether to encourage you
or me or the soaked wolves who cower at our feet
our voices assume a calm as weird
as the eye of some cosmic hurricane
that opens to reveal its own truth.

Numb and saturated by spray, it is now
I love you most, love your thick purple wrist
straining to hold the bird above hungry waves,
love the deft gentleness of your swollen hand
that cuts brutal knots without wounding the bird
who stares at you resolute as its barbed restraint.

When, finally, you saw through the last
twist of styrene, you fling the huge bird free.
It tucks oil black wings
to dive deep, then surfaces twenty feet out
to regard us before it plunges
back to the murky heart of the sound.

Amazed at the grit of survival, we are
stunned as any congregation touched
by near calamity, saved as that bird
putting watery distance between itself
and us as we paddle back to shore
above condemned rows of sea bass and all
the snared creatures we cannot see.

LOVE NOTE ON A MONDAY MORNING IN NORTH CAROLINA

Off to the airport again, you sail
away from home as you do each week,
owl-headed Odysseus bound
for the island of sorcery and soaring glass,
where a bear could be turned into a pig
on Times Square if he didn't watch his back.
This is just to say that there are black plums
ripening for you in the pewter bowl on our counter.
As if they could atone for the sin of separation,
the dogs hang their heads
in the baskets of their lonely paws
while I wait for you in the buttery sheets
of my suspended breath, figuring
balance on the tightrope of our dreams
without fear in air humid and alien
as rainy tarmac you now land on.   Stride out
into the concrete labyrinth, break
open the full bear bouquet of your life, know
the thread is strong that will lead you home,
where the plums are bursting their skins.

ANOTHER WIFE SEES HER LOVE OFF TO WAR

I'm not surprised I sliced my finger
after you left this afternoon.
The moon rises in its full fog of longing,
and I hear a vibrato of goodbyes like grenades
going off under my skin. In my purse
your cell phone takes messages
you won't hear for months.

My words walk into dreams
rattling their ankle cocoons that recall
the sweet tremble of wet wings
before they learned to fly. Now you fly
thousands of miles from my heart
that flutters off from the stench of its duties
to keep blood and bone alive, swollen
by an ache as acute as winter stars
driven under my fingernails.

Some cosmic joke this passion that strips
my skin to flap like prayer flags
in the complete loneliness of snow.
Where can ice edges melt when men drum
for revenge, and I am stuck again
in the swamp of their rhetoric, their need
to maim the long arms of desire?
A compass needle spun in the palm of history,
battles come true in grief's key of screams.

What skirmish do I need when my heart is set
to leap into the pyre of its longing, dreaming
fat as the moon that remembers the skin tent
flapping like hawk wings in desert wind,
the spin of me dancing before you ride off
with your warriors, the last tattoo
of your fingers on my cheek?

WE THOUGHT NO ONE COULD SEE US

Although it didn't freeze, the tulip tree flames, its
leaves as big as fiery umbrellas
plunging to the neighbor's late lawn, and I see
for the first time all summer, holes
in our privacy.
The illusion we've loved, that
we're alone and secret in the woods, instead
of backed up like a truck full of contraband
to a dull suburban development,
begins to unravel as we tilt away from sun.

Across the road, horses graze on humid grass,
neighbors we adore. They drift
like contented ghosts through morning fog
almost distracting us from the NPR commentator
who breaks news—in Fallujah our soldiers
have gunned down another Iraqi police squad
by mistake, police our forces trained
to rein in the chaos of our war
on terror.
    Friendly fire, the military names
this massacre of all eight officers, just like
the massacre of nameless scores
these months, although *friendly*
crashes like a mortar through the airwaves,
shatters the floor of the helpless kitchen we pace
while we wonder how we can paste all
those dying leaves back on our trees.

BLOSSOMING IN LILITH'S GARDEN

I pick wild cherries plump as the fire moon
as I walk the random borders
of my garden's full blooms—
fuchsia petunias that tongue
velvet Pasque flowers pulling themselves
erect as silk temples next to the blousy lips
of giant snapdragons, pink
cosmos in gauzy frocks, and
red geraniums lewd on green stalks.
Sky flaunts blue skin spread
wild as Lilith, Salome, and Bovary in their prime
opening luscious arms to lift
golden eagles, ravens, mountain
blue birds and vultures alike.
This heat-ticked season shouldn't be wasted.
I listen for my love's slow snores
storming our dreaming house and know
I want to be entered the way wind
bites into wildfire cracking through sage
or the way the sunset-bellied brook trout
strokes her entire body
into the muscular current to find upstream.
Dry earth longs for torrents, for
unbound knuckles of rain
to pound into it after months of sun.
And me? Today I am Lilith
open as a garden where insolent fruits
and heavy-breasted flowers shake their booty
above the snaking roots of trees.
Wrapped in a silk robe the color of wind
I pad inside from the barefoot yard, fertile
soil splaying my toes, wild cherries
staining my teeth.

FIGHTING THE COLD

Look at these hands, purpled by May's final
winter slap, wrinkled as rice paper, chilled
from eating cottage cheese and wind
that knifes through branches like a rapist
through lace. My clipped thumbnail is
my dad's aurora borealis of pale eggplant and tangerine,
Grandma's small fingers, tiny moons
white-rimmed and hard as the knuckle on a ghost.
Some days I believe I will never warm up.
Love has tucked its laughter behind metal clouds,
inside the entities of crystalline snow.
This morning, thinking it spring, I wrapped
the cord around the electric heater,
stowed it deep in the stone basement.

Oh stupid faith, like my friend said, I have a face
that feeds on false hope. Now falling
low as my blood pressure
late winter clouds razor the tips of new aspen
leaves, frost sweet alyssum and bleeding hearts.
But this poem is supposed to be about my hands
and the way they drop spoons when they're cold,
the way they can't hold their own warmth
and sometimes hurt so bad the cartilage screams.
My mother said warm heart, but I know
it's just bad circulation, the unwillingness of the heart
wounded too often to share a gush of new blood.

I remember the way my father's hand
clawed, middle finger drawn tight as a bowstring
to the palm by the stiff sinew, his inflexible will,
while grandma's remained graceful, young as a green flame.
Before it's too late and my fingers lock
around their empty globe of air, they must learn
the fine art of fire, to consume,
be consumed.

WILDFLOWERS
For Anna Petroska Jackinchuk (1894-1983)

I

I arrange cornflowers, brown-eyed Susans,
roadside purple rockets--
decades since you taught me their names.
      You said wind scoured words from your head,
blowing stronger each year.

Grandma, I remember asking
about the old country, red poppy fields and mountains
blue as aging veins,
cures boiled from mushrooms,
      and the times, coming home late, you hid
in river willows
      spying on a gypsy camp.
Dreaming of perfect love, you hugged
yourself against cold and rocked
to balalaikas and guitars, those firelit tongues,
wild as the icons in your mother's bedroom.

That dark pulse caught you early
one morning, when, instead of capping beer
in the family brewery, you climbed
onto blocks of straw-covered ice and
danced until you flipped
head-first to the skidding floor.
Unconscious days you dreamed
you were a wren tossed inside a storm.
When you woke, the wind began.

Did you think it was penance
when your mother sent you alone
and knowing no English
to be saved by America?
        Your sole welcome to Ellis Island
was a gust of Atlantic waves.

II

In Philadelphia you rolled cigars
then fled, strange wren, to sing
and dance in carnivals until you saw Grandfather's
fire-black eyes in his charmed face.
High-stepping, he was
your fairy tale Russian prince.

Remember yellow roses, amethyst
lilacs, kiss-me-over-the-garden-gate?
Their petals held no alien voice
but became the fluid language
you composed into a garden
when Grandfather betrayed
his promises of faith and lace.

Even as you planted the Peace Rose,
packing black soil around its waxy trunk,
he bootlegged whiskey from Canada,
bought long black sedans
and pearl-studded suits to win
women whose gorgeous faces
you weeded from nightmares.

His manic laughter was prohibition
that kept you at the stove over borscht,
babka, duck blood soup.

How you hated to sing
and dance for his Purple Gang friends,
that bloody mob that packed
the false walls of your house
with whiskey and bathtub gin, who used your sons
as innocent mannequins to foil police.

The story I savor is the final time
that Grandfather met you
at the front door, that leather strap
taut in his white knuckles
as you led your kids
back from the Saturday matinee.

Over the porch rail you shattered
a milk bottle, whispering
        Come on, Mister, now things must change.
Broken glass threatening his throat, he dropped
the belt, and from that day
you passed untouched.
You took in laundry, mopped
rich oak floors so you
could buy groceries
with your independent coins.
By that sweet rebellion
your children were fed.

Bullets tore the roots from your dreams
those long months Grandfather was shuttled
to prison for a murder no one could prove.
        On his last parole he beat
your youngest son, my father, then
backhanded him through the bleeding porch window.
Even his most furious screams could not
order his son back into the terrified house.

Hours before you got off work
Grandfather locked the kitchen doors,
blew out the pilot,
and suffocated the bloom of his swollen
sorrow in your stove.

III

Is it any surprise you warned me
about men? Warrior,
you had to stand your own ground, even
the time your second husband was so drunk
he couldn't recall
how whiskey drove anger
        when he split the kitchen table top
with a cleaver meant for you.
        Mowing the lawn he cut
the plush tongues of snapdragons,
fragile moss rose,
snow-on-the-mountain,
cursing stems and petals clogging his blades.

Complaints were as foreign
as I would become to you.
Memorizing your hands, weightless
and resilient as bird bones,
I came to say goodbye
You pointed to the magnolia opening the yard
with blossoms healing as your absolute laughter.
        So far north, you marveled
it survived so many winters
when hardier plants died.

I told you I was flying to mountains
I'd never seen, knowing
I had to cultivate other ground.
I tried to talk you into coming with me
but you repeated,
    Wildflowers can't be transplanted.
    I want to die in my own house.

Grandma, you loved best
dark petals,
       black marooned roses,
cinnamon deep azaleas.
The richest you fixed in my hair.
I still can't turn from your blue eyes
that tend a garden I could own.

There is no sound as loud as
this passing when you waved through the screen,
    I'll see you in the clouds
    when the wind stops.

RAMMING THE PORTUGUESE MAN-O-WAR ON OUR 14TH WEDDING ANNIVERSARY

For better or worse, we sweat through t-shirts
spiked with tropic heat and
black biting gnats as we walk to the beach
where brown pelicans
and Caspian terns tuck ice-colored wings
to crash beak first into breakers
blue as the backs of bottle flies. Ah,
        to forget
the thrombosis of thrown rods, our old blistered
Land Cruiser that bled out
all its oil yesterday afternoon
in Sonoran desert scald. To forget
the way we tossed
like car crash dummies inside
the broiling wrecker with no speedometer
that earned its name as it towed us
100 hallucinogenic miles to San Carlos.

All I want is to ride the tide of belief
that our luck will turn gold as a tooth and
our car will live so we can make it back
to Tucson.   Even baked sand stinks
as we wade, then dive into chuffing surf.

A breeze riffles the roll of waves that
tugs us away from sizzling shells, from the whine
of flies and panic over earthly disasters.

Off we paddle our separate ways, you
snorting like a bull seal as you snorkel
just beyond the pier and me, broken mermaid
breast-stroking for the bay's dark heart,
arms thrust through blood-warm crests and
pledging my future
        to this mindless watery marriage.

There is no warning rattle, no hiss
of wings, no quiver, no roil
just the startling sear abrupt
and electric as downed wires, bites
invisible as monofilament nets, that
inoculate my chest, the length of my arms
with angry mouths red as new smallpox scars
or rapid bursts of gunfire.

When I submerge, desperate, I am face
to face with the asphyxiated beauty
of a jellyfish, huge blue death mask, salient
cabbage or milky brain hinged
to toxic tentacles twenty feet or more
that float like translucent ribbons.

I backpedal, then pull deliberate fists
full of sea water all out for shore, but
even when I slog onto the beach
I can't escape the constellation of welts
that like immortal wasp stings or
guilt-slinging from an angry spouse, intensify
when exposed to air, mortifying my flesh.

Love, I scream you back
to the beautiful beach we trusted, through
the sea transformed to a terrorist attack
as shocking as the one confession of betrayal
we wait all our lives to receive.

Hurrying past sumptuous sprays of yellow bells
and maroon bougainvillea nodding
hallucinogenic as the siesta calm, you
guide me to the *farmacia*, bride pissed
as a soaked cat, needled by
venomous brine and sucking breath.

All the while your voice circles, reliable
as the hum of the earth believing
in its orbit around the sun, an analgesic
that repeats reassuring vows despite
unrelenting pain, the frenzied halos of biting flies,
our luck's pendulum on this charmed day
that swings out and back.

Sea of Cortez, Mexico

COLOPHON

Limited signed edition of 100 copies.

Designed by Carla Rozman.

Typeset in Adobe Garamond, designed by Claude Gara-
mond, a French type designer and founder; c.1480-1561.
One of the first punch cutters to work independently of
printers, Garamond perfected the design of roman type
and used it to replace the Gothic then commonly used.

Printed by Bookmobile, Minnesota.